Rousing the Machinery

Rousing the Machinery

POEMS BY
CATHERINE MACDONALD

THE UNIVERSITY
OF ARKANSAS PRESS
Fayetteville
2012

ISBN-10: 1-55728-979-4
ISBN-13: 978-1-55728-979-7

16   15   14   13   12   5   4   3   2   1

Designed by Liz Lester

⊛ The paper used in this publication meets the minimum requirements
of the American National Standard for Permanence of Paper for Printed
Library Materials Z39.48-1984.

LIBRARY OF CONGRESS CATALOGING-IN-PUBLICATION DATA

MacDonald, Catherine A. (Catherine Anna), 1957–
    Rousing the machinery : poems / by Catherine MacDonald.
        p.   cm.
    Includes bibliographical references.
    ISBN 978-1-55728-979-7 (pbk. : alk. paper)
    I. Title.
PS3613.A2713R68   2012
811'.6—dc23

                                    2011048816

For John, Sam, and Jacob

And in memory of my mother,
Anne Marie MacDonald, 1932–2010

Acknowledgments

I am grateful to the editors of the following publications who first published these poems, some in earlier versions or with different titles:

Babel Fruit—"A Family I Knew" ("Pinocchio in Africa"), "Appetite" ("Eccentric Orbit of the Moon"), and "BBC News"

Blackbird—"Rousing the Machinery," "Leda at Work in the World," "Transitions for Dancers When Dance Is No Longer an Option," and "Sweet Box"

The Cortland Review—"'You Are Loosed from Your Mooring,'" "Estranged Labor," and "Song of the Last Meeting"

Crab Orchard Review—"Blue Strobe"

Louisville Review—"Chevrolet Impala" and "'House-Hunters'"

Southern Indiana Review—"Notes on Prison" and "Weather Eye" ("Storm Season")

storySouth—"Load" and "Unreliable Narrator"

Tar River Poetry—"Teaching Myself to Sew"

Washington Square—"Grace" and "Empire and the Evangelical Sublime"

Some of the poems in this collection also appeared in the chapbook *How to Leave Home*, published by Finishing Line Press in 2009.

I would also like to express my appreciation to those who have generously supported my writing: the MFA program at Virginia Commonwealth University; the Sewanee Writers'

Conference; Ropewalk Writers Retreat; and Carole Weinstein and the Virginia Center for the Creative Arts for providing space and time to work on many of these poems.

Many thanks to Enid Shomer for her guidance and perceptive comments on my manuscript and to the staff at the University of Arkansas Press who turned that manuscript into a book.

My deepest thanks to those who have thoughtfully read and responded to these poems all along the way: David Wojahn, Claudia Emerson, Greg Donovan, Leslie Shiel, Kathy Davis, and Leslie Ratigan. Thank you for your insight, patience, and warm friendship.

And I am forever grateful to my husband John Ulmschneider, whose faith in me made this work possible.

CONTENTS

Rousing the Machinery

Called back in wonder,

the strangeness, the story endlessly told any life unfurls,
causal chains of small decisions,
almost random, those accidents of grace or luck.

—LYNDA HULL, "RED VELVET JACKET"

ONE

◆ ◆ ◆

Grace

In this raw corner of a no-rank town, rusting
swing sets wobble under the weight of fierce

children as thunderstorm torrents ride pin-
straight alleys down the backsides

of backyards. When they think no one
is looking, my brothers pee on the alley

storm-grates. This is my footpath to Grace,
seventh house on the left. An air conditioner,

the only one for blocks, sweats and sighs
in her jammed-open front window as August

simmers. Grace is abandoned. A monkey balances
on her bare right shoulder, simpers and shrieks,

grips her dull blonde hair with an infant's avid
hands. It's a gift from her ex, an airman late

of Saigon. Outside her door frothy mimosas
waft scent over the dying lawn as she ties one on.

Don't bother with her, my mother scolds.
She's a drunk. But I knock anyway, every day.

Drawn by the monkey's cry and the air conditioner's
cold invitation, I face Grace on her front stoop.

As soaring jets rope the morning sky, Grace
raises her glass and invites me inside.

Weather Eye

At the dinged sink in the dark kitchen, I watch
      my father pour bottled water, warmed
            on the gas grill, and glistening

shampoo over my mother's head. He rubs
      away the crackle of old hairspray,
            the scent of cigarette smoke

from her fading red curls. The power has been out
      for days. I cross the threshold of that
            tenderness into another storm

season when blows passed between them as recklessly
      as cars pass under traffic lights on the blink,
            flashing *stop—go—slow.*

Then the squall slipped off shore, and the river in gray
      sheets went back to bed. When my mother
            phoned to tell me, *A stroke is what explodes*

in the head, not the heart, this is what I remembered—
      oldest child, restless eavesdropper—
            all night we drove through snow.

From the backseat where children sleep,
      I heard my father say, *There was a time*
            when nothing was between us. He turned

from the road to my mother, their youngest
child, untroubled, drifting off
in the seat between them.

Indian-Style, In Front of the Tube

On Wednesday nights we sit for *The Rifleman*,
      then for Fred and Ethel, Lucy and Ricky,
            for little Ricky, too, like our own

little Ricky, youngest of five, redolent of baby
      shampoo, plump in my lap, hot from his bath.
            (It's still years before his prison term, cable,

the internet, and his own silent son; but it's swimming
      towards us. We'll crest one wave, then another.)
            But tonight it's television. Of course,

we think our mother is just like Lucy,
      only not funny, and our father just
            like Ricky, only not Cuban and he can't play

a note. Lucy's feisty, always in a scrape
      with him, the hot-tempered blade,
            bongo-battering hunk. Can you imagine

him in Havana—the music thick in his head—that pout,
      his wavy black hair—or swimming the Florida Straits,
            conga strapped to his back?

This is the life: bowl of pistachios,
      peanuts, and popcorn as we watch Ricardo
            rise from the waves, storm Manhattan,

and light the ladies' cigarettes at Club Babalu. But poor
      Lucy's got some 'splaining to do as she carves
            charred chicken and dresses down

the kids. You know, it's all part of a long
      letting-go, a rerun in pings and flutters
            in the crankcase of the brain,

you monkey you.

Blue Strobe

      I was almost arrested once, an open
bottle of St. Pauli Girl cooling my palm
      in a Charlottesville alley. The cop? He yelled,
mostly at the man I was with. Sometimes
      it's good to be a girl when boys hide out,

assemble forts. It's not all innocent fun,
      I know, but it is fun, slipping stoned
down a steep drive, past the loading
      dock, in through a door too warped
to close. The old hospital is half demolished,

      and they've broken in here before, drawn
to its echoes and stuccoed ruin. You couldn't break
      it anymore than it's already broken. In the chapel
on the fifth floor, they've fashioned
      a space. This is where they're caught

spattering walls and pews with gold spray paint—
      leftover from last year's Spanish project,
a cardboard model of the Alcazar of Segovia—
      the carpet littered with Raisinets
as if life were a movie matinee.

      As if life were an excursion
to the library, these are the books
      they brought there: *The Rum Diaries,*

Rumi, Chomsky, *Star Fighter,* Calvin
  and Hobbes. Just what is it

boys need? I know it's not in their book-
  bags or in the deep pockets
of their cargo pants. This life has a soundtrack;
  it loops through wire and plastic buds
rooted in the ear: Belle and Sebastian,

  the Zombies, Johnny Cash, all singing
about the demise of childhood while a signal
  from a joystick rag-dolls virtual victims
in a simulated Ardennes Forest, circa 1944,
  or Vice City's ferocious streets, circa 1983,

or an animated NeverWinter, circa
  forever and ever. So oaks wilt and wounded
elms doff their crowns, which don't sit lightly
  on the spindly necks of winter wrecks—
no leaves yet. These shut-fast

  houses beneath bent trees, that's what
I asked for, square above a racing river,
  the velocity of its current calculated
remotely by strobe and transmitted
  via satellite to engineers who wait

restlessly to wring meaning from raw
     data. Six boys, hands flat on the hood
of an unmarked police car, circa 2008.
     Its blue strobe is the river's pulse at its sharpest
bend, wildest branch, and highest bluff.

Notes on Prison

We love our brother
so we visit him in prison
where he (Possession with Intent)
and Carlos (Manslaughter)
are buddies, cellmates. They lift
together, share shampoo
and the sci-fi novels our sister brings.
Carlos is a man with a business plan,
an artist from Jalisco. He shows us
his sketchbook: the Basilica
of the Virgin of Zapopan, patroness
of epidemics and thunderstorms. His sister
strumming the *vihuela*. A man's open palm.
But here, it's reverse paintings on glass
for sale or barter—maybe Disney
for baby or one of the Bible's bad boys
for mama, or your sweetheart's
face copied from a wrinkled photo.
No photo? No problem—just her name,
then, leaking sapphire tears
over a bulging heart, your name
in hard black letters in the middle.
So Sundays we bear tubs of fried chicken
and bags of doughnuts to Deerfield
Prison for Men. We get to know
the guards. Pines rise above

the stucco and tin, the din
of women wrapped around thin boys
or thickset men, who must say it now,
say it fast, say it loud:
The lawyer called (or didn't)
No, your father, he won't come here
and *I can't forgive or forget or forgo*
any of it. Of course, this was years ago.
We took a few pictures. We took our children
to see their uncle, who didn't say much, just
carried leftovers back to his cell for Carlos,
whose faraway family thought he was dead.

Sunrise with Voices

Do you remember the song in the yard?
Was it wind-tunnel and jet howl?
Or bird-call at dawn, the low vowels
of a mourning dove, its forage of the lawn?

I had a morning paper route, fenders fitted
out with two baskets, and I was strong,
pedaling dark streets, morning paper my song,
pitched hard, end over end, a crazy flight,

fast and long. That summer my father
worked two jobs, days racing the flight line,
nights chasing a mop, all to feather our nest,
the tidy brick ranch with a trim lawn, where we

wrestled and rushed to grow up. Bird-early,
I'd hear him before I saw him, pass him
as he headed home, car windows rolled down,
Merle Haggard, ragged and ruined on the radio.

He'd join in, his fine voice, deep and drunk. Weaving
wagon, jangle and din of mandolin, pedal steel.
Simple licks. Damn the sleeping house, its angry
wife within—this was the song in the yard.

Patron Saint of the Toothache

Each October and April the poor children of Boston are seen
for a nickel at the Forsyth Clinic, baby teeth rotted by hot tea—

creamy and sweet—and penny candy, filched by the fistful
after Mass. What wailers these are, subject to the trembling

ministrations of the young dental students—*fill this one, pull that one*—
those rapt pupils of decay and defect, grinding clean the gaping

caries and crooked incisors. Do you see that boy, smaller, more
terrified than the rest, his mouth pried open with wads of cotton?

Bad teeth like his papa before him, he hears his mother say, and remembers
the night when his father, swearing on the eye-teeth of St. Apollonia,

pulled his own bad tooth from his own aching jaw, staunching
the blood with a bleached diaper from the baby. You know this child,

vertebrae stacked straight, intersecting the hard vault of the skull,
made upright, to walk, to run, eyes ahead, never looking back.

for my father

Chevrolet Impala

i.

Sleepless, my father roams the house, pausing
in each of our rooms: two sturdy boys in pine
bunks, three girls in parallel single beds—
our blankets knit with Degas dancers fixed in place—
pale backs, arched feet, unwinding chignons.
A girl's nylon slip is a slick spill on cold linoleum
between two beds. He stoops and folds it
into the dresser-drawer's narrow hold. Evenings,
smoke curls from cigars lit with a silver lighter
his father left in the ashtray of the Chevrolet Impala
years ago. It sank on leaking tires in a Roxbury alley,
its chassis silvering in snow, rusting in April's humid
breezes. Summer, its luster faded to citrine.
A spiral of gingko leaves cloaked it in fall.

ii.

A dumb-ass lobsterman from Prince Edward Island,
my grandfather never drove his adopted city's
narrow streets, but anointed that Chevy's interior
with pipe smoke and the rattle of the *Boston Globe*,
guarding it from vagrants, fools, and family
while my father flew solo over Laos and the South
China Sea. On tiptoe, we children inspected the car,
our five faces bright in windows shut tight against

us. Soon the family reunited, headed south,
my father again at the wheel: past the Fens,
through Providence, over the rocky Mystic and wide
Delaware, down the unresisting Eastern Shore
to kiss the smooth lip of the Chesapeake.
Behind us, the old man, cast off in the city again.

iii.

There are no photos of my father
and his father, both seasick at the rail,
on the auto-ferry from Bar Harbor, Maine,
to Yarmouth, Nova Scotia. I've imagined these
travelers into this trip, scripted their dialog.
If the old man asks, *How far left to go?*
His son might answer, *What else is owed?*
Just this, I would tell them: sum and substance,
gist and core. On shore, I steer their silence
over island roads, bind them to cold ocean,
join them to no women, no children, to plow
sea fog, plant wasp husk, and reap stone.
All night, the Impala rolls with the waves, a deft
machine that knows no sleep, no sleep, no sleep.

Estranged Labor

This is the work of the house.
You are in charge of the grass,
I am in charge of the plates.
You stalk live game, every pursuit
a compromise, the pale interior
absolving the elements outside.
You fight the numberless leaves.
I slaughter the hens and keep
their pimpled flesh from the hound.
This is the work of the house.
You salt the slug. I wrestle the twisted
limb from the blazing tree. Consider
the sweep of carpet moss, the lure
of a wire worm snaking the drain.
Tail curled above muscled hock,
the gazehound wakes from uneasy
sleep, her eyes on the spilled
drawer, the door ajar.

"House-Hunters"

Where are we? Whose house is this? And who is the sleeper?

—EMERSON AT LONGFELLOW'S FUNERAL

Just before she drifts off, oxygen cannula
delivering its sibilant flow, my mother observes

that tonight's young couple on our favorite show
hasn't the right energy for the hunt: she's a whiner,

he's a lunk. It will elude them, she says, the sexy master
suite, granite kitchen facing a fenced backyard perfect for two

enviable dogs, stand-ins for children still to come.
Will it be the ranch or the cape? Close-in or far out?

Round each cul-de-sac, they'll wonder: Can you see
yourself here—rooted in place like a nerve or a nail?

Lately, my mother rarely leaves the house, so we spend
the day on family photos: Easter and Christmas,

baskets and bows, year after year her children in rows
crowding the stoop or circling the pine, elbow-to-elbow

in a lengthening line. There are a few of her, too:
sweeping a room or at the stove, one baby or another

astride her hip, always a cigarette burning
between her lips. At house number 3, I wake her.

It's time to choose. She slips her glasses down her nose.
Even a fool can see how this will go.

At the Jefferson Pools

These springs are very much resorted to in spite of a total
want of accommodation for the sick. Their waters are
strongest in the hottest months. . . .

—THOS. JEFFERSON, NOTES ON THE STATE OF VIRGINIA

I try to imagine my mother taking these waters,
comfortably naked, silent. But she's too sick—
impossible to travel so far—and more modest
than anyone here, than anyone I've ever known.
Now, near the end of her life, she feels ugly,
no longer keeping house or sleeping with my father.

      I make her visit the doctor, a man her own age,
who asks her to take off her shirt, her bra, to lift up
her left breast so he can slip his stethoscope
beneath. While I watch from the door, his eyes—
blue like hers—focus on some middle distance. His skin,
like hers, is mottled and no longer smooth. His head,
cocked to that rhythm and riff, shakes. Her heart,
clenched and worn, her breast in her hand.

I've read that near the end, ill and weak,
Jefferson was bored by the baths. Yet, weary,
heat hard at his back, he departed again
for the high country, and its three springs—
the warm, the sweet, the white—carried over
new roads made smooth by forest animals

and trailing hunters, whole families on foot,
pushing handcarts, moving west.

      Imagine this: from a ridge a buck in full velvet
eyes the carriage-and-four that bears the sick man
to the baths. He has vowed no unction of mercury, no
tincture of poppy—instead, the old remedy. He will drift
above the stony bottom, aching and cold, let the waters
wash what stings, what is sore as hobnail rubbing heel.

How to Leave Home

i. *ars domestica*

In our rectangular ranch house, crowding
      its square lot, we were puppies in a box,
mere instinct, wriggle, pulse, five of us,
      turned out daily with a tissue
and clean socks. Table-rappers at a séance,
      Morse code operators on the graveyard shift,
we signaled in taps and thumps
      through the bedroom walls, our dreams
a kind of manned space flight. Moving low
      over rough waters, we dropped to wrestle
a giant squid or two, surfacing
      safe and strange in our deep diver suits.

ii. the odds

We outnumbered them, but they outweighed us,
      bringing to the table clear advantages,
such as height and considered opinions
      on diet, democracy, and the quality
of mercy. Five versus two. You calculate
      the odds. Our appetites and longings
overwhelmed them; they often gave in
      to despair. What we didn't tell, they
discovered. What we thought we'd concealed,
      they already knew. Memory follows

no pattern; events do not repeat
        precisely. This is a simple calculation,
an arithmetic of expectations.

iii. what pets teach children

The polydactyl cat—part totem, part
        tormentor—knew my sister, seventeen,
was pregnant before she did. Its cross-eyed
        gaze, disdainful, its haughty retreat
down the dark hall. And the hognose snake
        in the laundry-room terrarium? Played dead
when it all turned ugly and planes crashed
        into bungalows, my brother's drug money,
vacuumed up from under his bed. My father,
        his fists into the wall, then on his son's head.
A brawl, rattling windows, slamming doors.
        The wide, flat bay—our fitful friend—
slightly sick, slick with oil.

iv. east wind, rain

It's not such a rare story to have a child
        who breaks your heart. Or maybe you break
his and then you both run away from home.
        You've got the keys to the car, the secret
code, access to all the loot—blips and gaps
        in the account, everything vanishing in a blink.
Later there's a gasp, the lapse, the photos gone.

v. bedsprings

Harvested at day's end from swampy woods,
        we crept from bed to bed all night long,
making the signs for fire, flight, ocean, air.
        Our motto: the plane of the wing and the wing
of the plane, the only constants. Each night
        my youngest brother at our bedroom door,
pillow at his chest like a shield. He faced
        three narrow beds against the windowless
wall, lined up like bull pines along a straight
        road: our bower—identical spreads, one flat
pillow each, bleached sheets over our tender toes.

vi. The roots of the holly and the story of flight

The roots find steady work cracking
        the sidewalk, a jagged line
pointing to my brother, who hacks
        the tree with a handsaw. He hums,
grinding into green wood, splintering
        what won't rot, won't burn.
The leather palms of our father's old gloves
        are stiff armor against the pointed leaves,
short spines, and rough bark of the species.

Search Engine

Let me describe what I have that is yours:
a bent photo of your mother, a man's

wool coat over her housedress, curlers
under her tight kerchief. She reaches

from the lake shore to a cop who has rowed
through the slush with your family's unlucky

collie shivering in the keel of his canoe.
She will wrap the dog in a blanket, carry her

home, then smooth the animal's rough coat
with a brush from her beauty shop.

This photo made the wires
in the wet, drifting winter of 1966, a year

before your father turned the collie out
onto one of the county's empty roads,

before he packed your mother off
to the state hospital, you and your sister

to an aunt. When we were nine, I loved your life
as if it were my own, and now I want to find you,

so I enter your husband's name
in the search engine. The first click delivers

a gallery of butterflies: fiery skipper,
whirlabout, grey hairstreak. The next,

a catalog of campaign collectibles,
ferrotype and jugate: We Want Willkie.

Hail to the thieves. Come home, America.
Then his latest undertaking—

ruddy ducks, puffins, coots, and stilts,
snapped on bright waterways

from Newfoundland to Texas. He roams,
shoots, returns each spring when the pond

you watch from your window cracks
and thaws. I've found you under the covers

in a fading coal-town. Risperdal and lithium sigh
from the hollow of your guitar. From deep winter

you write back to me: *Gardening catalogs sprout
under the bed. January's ice skates wait*

pigeon-toed on the floor, blades still sharp.

Unreliable Narrator

It's the nature of memory—not linear,
but like sparks shooting from a fire

or a familiar shape smuggled in,
promising something tender: a kiss

on the forehead, the cheek, the chin
to chasten and chagrin. I recast

your mother as your sister. The suicide?
A freak accident. A long marriage?

No, years wasted, alone. No children?
Just two cats, uncomplicated and clean.

That swamp-set trailer is somehow
now a quarter-acre lot, only a block

from the murmuring bay—and the deserted
back road to the beach? It's a cul-de-sac,

where we never played girly games or permitted
girls to enter. Did I mention Kama Sutra

powder tossed over your shoulder, snowdrift
clouding a mirrored tray? I am someone

who remembers everything you forgot
to mention, but don't depend on me.

TWO

❖ ❖ ❖

Leda at Work in the World

In the swelling wind before a September
storm, I tow my two boys on one last
loop around the lake as the season's last
fishermen stash sunspot and shimmering

bass in dull metal buckets. Bait boxes,
butts, and soggy branches bump
the slick bank, while offshore a mute
swan thrashes the waves with wings

half-spread, its mate in wild orbit
nearby. My sons ask, *What's wrong
with that bird?* I point: *It's that fisherman—
look.* A barelegged angler anchors

the shallows where he wrestles and curses
his snake-necked catch, his barbed
hook piercing the swan's bill. We join
a crowd gathering on shore, gesturing

and muttering as rising gusts ruffle the water.
Then, from among us, she strides past,
sheds her sandals, steps from shore.
Thigh-deep, she stills the bird in a deft

embrace, works the hook from its bill.
Frees it. Swan and mate wheel away
as she climbs the bank, wrings the lake
from her clothes, bends, buckles her sandals.

Brown braid, sunglasses, stern and shy, she
turns from the lake-edge, where my sons,
forgetting as boys will, seize up sticks
to beat back storm clouds in the water.

Rousing the Machinery

The tygers of wrath are wiser than the horses of instruction.
　　　　　　　　　　　　　—WILLIAM BLAKE, *THE MARRIAGE*
　　　　　　　　　　　　　　　　　OF HEAVEN AND HELL

i.

Observe the perpetual boy, as one
with the pop-eyed crowd. He's come
to see the King's menagerie: camel, bear,
leopard, lion, *tyger:* stripe over stripe,
swinging its heavy head with each sullen
step. He notes the fixed pit of its pupil,
the eyes' bulge and slow blink. Who will extol
this captive, pacing the round tower room?
Who will grind its bones for luck, pluck
stiff whiskers for a paintbrush, rend fat
for an aphrodisiac? Who will inhale
scent of musk, tang of urine soaked
in stone, sing, *Marvelous, its assets?*
A boy.

ii.

This morning in Raleigh's exurban flank,
I watch the bad boys of Selma
Alternative High School craft paper wasps.
They loft them across the bedlam
of the classroom to where the *tyger,* perfect-
bound, sleeps in my hands. With a stroke,

a stroke, a stroke, the machinery is roused
and in the corner of the classroom,
above our heads, gangly wasps disgorge wood
to make paper. Watch: the miracle
occurs in a vessel, an enclosure, in a lidded pot
on a hot stove, in a woman's body
where a child grows, or in the insect
jaw, ganglia, and lobe.

Appetite

After a semester away, my son is observing
Ramadan, fasting from sunrise to sunset.
I'm a fucking feckless aristocrat, he tells me,

as we cruise the grocery store aisles, a setting
he finds neither raw nor rough enough
for a man's life. We toss into the cart what

we cannot resist: tomatoes out-of-season,
polished apples, lemons stamped Sunkist
in celestial blue. Is it enough? I cannot see yet

how his uneating will lead him from hunger
to hunger. Will he find his face in the bright
curve of a spoon poised above a bowl—

like a boy's in Tikrit or Darfur? I offer hearts
of romaine and blood oranges, marbled meats
to coax, to claim the appetite, the universal wolf.

Load

The riggers arrive at eight, one squat,
the others lean as bamboo. Tough,
too, they laugh, *You need a size 6 hat
and a 44 chest to do this work.*

Beneath the porch and through
a trapdoor is the entrance to our basement
where the drowned washer and dryer, cold
furnace, rest in rusty puddles of weeks-old
rainwater. From the steps, I watch the men
eye the shapes, calculate the weight
of what must be removed.

Thick and beautiful knots
of heavy rope, the geometry of eyebolt
and derrick, pulley, tackle, and sling—
I call to my son, a balky boy asleep
in the smallest room at the top of the house,
Come down and see.

But he sleeps through the morning
while the men frame rough pine on site,
then balance the shifting load above
their shoulders as they shout,
Away!

Ambuscade

On my way to the kitchen—early,
on the second day of snow—I notice
the photo askew on the wall: winter
squall in black and white, ice packed
hard; a child's swing caught aloft,
and in the center, a smeared oval of light.
Street lamp? Falling star? It arrived
years ago on a Christmas card, matte

print taped to pale paper. I framed
everything then, and now everything
is the snow—how it harrows sleep,
sunk in its shift of cloud and blow.
If I took the photo out of its frame,
I could recover the sender, her message,
her name or pass on, let the storms bury
us both within, without.

This Is a Small God Whose Face I Saw

Handcuffed, maybe seventeen, she shuffles
into the emergency room's winking fluorescence.
Pregnancy has swelled her, ankles to cheeks, inflated
her Juvenile Detention Center jumpsuit, gassed-fruit

orange, a shade that flatters no one. She's with a cop,
a loud woman, who leans into the nursing station
and shrugs: *This girl don't know which one the daddy.*
In the triage line beside me, my husband: *Just don't*

look. We're each slotted a spot, this girl and me, thin
curtain between us. What a pair. I weep, she bleeds.
I bleed, she weeps: *Knock me out and take it away.* Twin
mounds in twin beds, we're tethered to machines

that sound the depths, though I cannot fathom face,
foot, or femur in that dark harbor. Her baby flexes
inside her, heart strong, with lungs still flat
and moist as laboratory specimens. We labor

while volunteers offer—*Ice chips? Tylenol?*—
and then withdraw. I hear the cop: *Getting a baby*
out is like a scrap with a ghost. Just think of this like
a roller coaster ride, once it starts up, you can't get off.

Sweet Box

Gadwall, pintail, wood duck—ecstatic swimmers
      in the cold current. The retriever's mouth
is suited to such prizes; its temperament,
      to mark and tremble on command; its coat,
to shed river; its movements, unlimbered
      and effortless as the current passing its
banks. Once two hundred soldiers crouched
      here above the torrent, hidden in ditches
and redoubts, this bluff a blanket folded
      above the flood. Sweet box flanks these fragile
earthworks, an arching scaffold of honey-
      musk. I climb the slope into its scent, lose
sight of the dog, come up on the old fort
      again, rinsed by river and rain, rain

and river. On the face of it, the past
      is a blank. Nine ounces, eleven inches,
nineteen weeks gestation—she will die
      in my arms, laboring to breath. But first
there is sweet box, winter's balm, improbable,
      flowering at the doctor's door. I wait
where the plant makes scent, as in December
      half-light a Swede savors rose-scented broth,
or a florist, under ballasts of light,
      resists the subtle stink of baby's-breath,

dreams impossible blue roses, uncrated,

     stripped of thorns. I wait, just shy of the door,
its pneumatic sigh and polished glass. Freighted.

     Fetus-on-board. Baby-in-tow. Eating-

for-two. Human-in-utero. Which genes

     make fragrance, and at what cost? Which make
my body fail its course, weary in its cramp,

     its bloody loss, all that tepid February?
Pouch empty this trip, the hunter drains his

     thermos, nurses a sputtering outboard
to shore, retriever quiet in the hull.

     Is this the most miserable of the hunter's
pursuits? To troll the cold river, gun cocked,

     alert for the sudden snap of muscular wings—
like a catch in your throat—moving upstream,

     following the dark riverbank? Twilight
marks passage over each bulge of the tilted globe,

     and it is twilight that drives the hunter home.

BBC News

The Queen's composer has ruffled feathers
after police found the body of a swan at his home.
            —"BBC: One-minute World News"

With a crook used for sheep-herding,
he ravels the swaying body of a whooper swan
from the power lines, its bulk still,
bill cracked. He'll make a stew of it—
dark meat, lean after a Scottish
winter—with stinging onion
and coarse pepper. From each breast
he slices clean its wing, hangs
them in the windy garden to dry.

November, and the last banded birds
move over the island like voices rising
over a single line of music. He envisions
a Nativity pageant, the island's slow boy—
as much pitied as loved—is the angel
Gabriel, whispering,
            First Elizabeth,
                    now you, Mary—
as the swan's wings unfurl above his shoulders.

Meditation on a Cape Sewn Badly

by me, your mother, for you, O difficult one,
a black satin cape, crooked seams, wicked red

lining, your hair smoothed back, wax fangs
flashing, lips ruby and wet with slick gloss.

Halloween night and trees rattle leaves in a breeze.
We hit the streets. A few doors down, the neighbor's

blind dog—one glass eyeball and a stitched-
shut socket—sports an angel's tinseled halo

and silver wings. She's facing down a prancing
pirate who pats her head fast and hard. The dog

squeezes shut her lid over the mock-eyeball
and snaps. Charging pirate and dog-seraph, you

brandish your cape over them both
as Dracula himself might have—

bite forsaken. O ruined angels of murky impulse
and yearning, *Listen to these, the children of the night.*

What music they make!

Some Mothers Ask

*"Prescription for the blues—Omega-3s, protein every
couple of hours, shower in AM, seek sunlight. And don't
forget to exorcise."*

—POSTING FROM AN ONLINE
POST-PARTUM DEPRESSION FORUM

Some mother's cell phone bawls with a baby's cry.
Yes, a howl like an infant's wails from her handset

in the frozen food aisle. Curious, I think, how that signal
spirals off a spiky tower rising in the guise of a fir,

orb spider spinning witlessly in its counterfeit
boughs. Gone are the restraints of botanically

correct foliage, shoots and root, bud and bloom.
Color riot, leaf rot, the fussy rigor of each season?

No longer relevant. Some mothers ask, *What kind of baby
is this? How will I know if it loves me—me, it?*

This longing, like the ache in the gut of an exile,
who reaches the summer saltwater line to find

only knotweed and goosefoot, skiff drifting
towards a false cape, many sea-miles away.

❖   ❖   ❖

After each miscarriage, it's new mothers who move me
most. I find them in grocery store lines wheeling a cart

half-full, mewling infant sunk in a sling, in restaurants,
shy, nursing through a hurried meal. I know mother-

hunger and baby-lust are yoked to the body-ox—
but what match fires that slow fuse? Every night I dream

of catastrophe, and each day carry out one useful chore.
No more sticky kitchen shelves. No oily imprint of the collie

on the dining room floor. My shallow drawers hold
armloads of homely objects, each with its deep intention

to pierce or measure out. A tiny fork. Hollow-handled
medicine spoon. Look—six scallop shells—a wedding gift,

cradles for sinew and bone. We use them as scoops, as ashtrays.
Repurposing, it's called.

❖   ❖   ❖

The milk bank nurse arrives each Tuesday
to find me attached to the pump, wrapped

in my husband's robe, leaning into whir and hum
as ounces of thin blue milk drip into a germ-free jar,

and in my freezer, sterile plastic cups, labeled
with date and hour. I am wet nurse to some mother's

daughter or son—a crack-baby served by prescription,
the infant of a mother with implants or AIDs, an infant

fostered. Odds-breaker, are you sister or brother? What if
that lost child slips out from the past, taps your shoulder,

asks you to dance? You, of course, oblige—loving best
what is just past reach, this *rara avis*, driven

from branch to branch, trailing the flock. For you, then,
this surplus, the hind-milk and fore.

Wasps in the Kitchen

It is warm again, and over the course of a morning
they emerge: fragile and torpid, bent like the very old,
two wasps in my kitchen. The first lingers near
a window, and over him I place a long-grown child's

sippy cup, once yellow as the sun, before moving
on to sweep from beneath the toaster the second wasp.
It clings to the rag I shake into the yard. Then I lift
the cup from over the first. No longer alarming,

he dreams of repeal and recision, of solving the plight
of a drone, a doomed suitor, whose drowsy
and expectant queen cannot banish this cold fog
wrapping the house, patient, persisting past noon.

"You Are Loosed from Your Mooring"

This is the pelican's view of the bay: fast-tack
of sails, stroke of a flock in flight, wind-reel
over water as schools silver the surface.
Imagine the bell of the jellyfish adrift, sea-ice
in August, wind-driven, tide-locked. Go

where shadows go, to the northeast corners,
above doorways, near chimneystacks. They buried
smooth stones here, for conjuring, sewing needles,
polished bone, a baby's tooth: the common-stuff
of a slave. Terns now dive the clotted creek and cedar

swamp, skirt sterile oyster reefs. Fair skies whirl
in from the west in homage to the night heron,
a nest robber, with its savage habit of tender
plunder. From stubbled fields, a blue tarp blusters,
wild over water, *an apostrophe to the moving multitude.*

THREE

◆ ◆ ◆

Empire and the Evangelical Sublime

Here is one way to navigate the world:
make mental maps from raw data.
Envision a grid of imaginary lines,
horizontal and vertical, fixed
at right angles on the flat likeness
of a sphere. Call it intersection, collusion,
or collision. I call it domestic
violence when it happens
in my own backyard. It's 1587.
It's Jesuits on the James. Smallpox
on a blanket in raw winter rain. I ask
myself: coincidence or conspiracy?
Or an accident of an entirely different
sort? I see the shocked expressions
of outrage trembling in four corners
of the room. With a compass rose
between my teeth, I orbit
the traffic rotaries of a flat earth.
As I said, this is one way to navigate
the world. Later, on an out-of-the-way
continent, I wrestle in the winner's circle
for relics, then devise a costume
appropriate for the weather: suitable
badges, bone buttons, hooks
to facilitate closure.

Untidy Geographies

Blonde, blue-eyed, she bikes to his corner
near Tiananmen Square every day for weeks, dropping

into a squat to watch him stroke a dragonfly above a pale
peony, a rabbit in quick grass. Once his brush slipped—

an errant splash of ink at the edge—and she got it for almost
nothing. Scorpions, starfish, strawberries on a skewer—

Good trade for poor work, he says. Fixed on thick rice paper, goldfinches
flicker through bamboo, mounted then and there

on blue silk—his bright chop in the corner—the painting
packed away at once. For twenty years, she kept it in the dark

beneath her bed, tight scroll in a red-lettered tube, forgetting
Mao's teeth blackened on posters, Hershey's and coffee

at the American Friends Hotel, the young soldiers' round-eyed
agitation, her own long letters home.

Russian Studies

Not spring yet, and we resent her quick
unburdening of each decade into our
spiral-bound notebooks. Inevitable
as the horde's wild advance on the dirt-
yoked peasant, she delivers the unpronounceable
patronyms of scoundrel and soldier, flashes
faded slides of tractors rusting into the black
dirt of Ukrainian fields. Stalin's *sovkhoz*
gone to seed. In March, hair loosened, sweater
cast aside, she weeps openly—*Don't worry,*
don't worry—over Red Army tanks, halted
on the banks of the Vistula in 1944,
the Polish Home Army crushed
as the bear winked, then yawned. In April
she looks up from the lectern: Russia turns
to her poets for the truth. Mandelstam,
Tsvetaeva, Blok—*Wind-the-slasher!*
Frost no better! At ten paces you can't hear
our words. She sighs. Akhmatova—*muse*
of keening, sorrow's sour wine—loved
not for her long nose or close-set eyes
but for an *inner flame.* Leningrad, 1966: a slide
of her funeral, casket open to winter wind.
The dead poet surrounded by young men.
Brodsky, she indicates, in a flapping trench coat
above a good-looking corpse. We turn

then to geography: winter's pinched
sun and forced idleness, the forests' riches—
beeswax, honey, ermine. And the nation's stories?
Always in need of translators. *And you,*
she chides us, *you will keep good notes.*

RAF Station, Norfolk, England, April 1940

Night the deep pocket
a thread running through it
    with no more heft than a strand

of hair knotted in the seam
    or a feather caught aloft
or wings in raveled motion

    above the rooftops
while England sleeps
    the radar-man tracks *angels*

months before the first bombs
    will arrive with whistle and whine
hundreds of greylag geese

    grown fat for long flight
move over his screen
    into the dark gap.

Yokota Airbase, Japan, 1961

Clouds arrive all morning from long ago
he recalls the lacquered discs of an abacus
      under his five-year-old fingers clicking

sums how many birds on the commissary
      lawn how many clothes-pins in mother's apron
pocket how many wings, tails, spin above

      but only three tiger's eyes rest on the sill nearby
spilled colors of that morning's arithmetic
      those glass marbles round and hard as the world.

A Family I Knew

Pinocchio listened very thoughtfully. He had never expected
that in Africa he was to hear so many disagreeable truths,
and he was on the verge of weeping.

—Eugenio Cherubini, *Pinocchio in Africa*

In Sierra Leone Emile scraped peanuts from sand,
ferried diamonds cut rough, scooped sweet potatoes
into burlap sacks. Tonight, in Virginia, he sighs—

Harmattan—Saharan silt aloft in the world's
thrusting heart. This much he knows: *The child*
militias stand in for us all. The hard killings are where I go

when I'm alone. A wanderer at work in the kitchen
of a family whose dining room commands a grand
view of the James, Emile—desert import, dessert server,

refugee—assists Ellen, stooped and reserved, damaged
young granddaughter of the resident grandee. Emile and Ellen
dance a strange two-step, silent yet attuned, twin damselflies

on a banker's brow, and together, serve us dinner in three
courses. Plant, animal, and mineral: wilted spinach,
tender veal on platinum-kissed Limoges. Emile's gold tooth

sparks in the candled light of the room. Later he wipes up,
serves coffee in delicate cups of Wedgwood Black Basalt,
while Ellen joins the table-talk—the family at the river,

ski trips to Gstaad, the farm above Oyster Bay. Each story
a photo without her in it. In the kitchen Emile pauses,
elbow-deep at the porcelain sink. This much he knows:

Sanctuary—a veil to wrap around you, child-god unmasking
the world. It's the clanging together, the swinging apart,
what's cleaved and then whole. Sanctuary—it arrives in disguise.

Geographies of Affect and Emotion

Burning hills are tipped with ash and the equatorial ocean
rocks birds and bodies as pale sharks churn through currents
of spilled fuel, fuselage. The neural hardware of the viewer

blazes at a speed past believing. I've read that somewhere
in California scientists count heartbeats and breaths, measure
the capillaries' dilation and pressure of jaw muscles clenched

against our spectacle: skein of interstate, bungalow
and jacaranda, landfill, oil derrick, triple-purpose high-rise,
sunflowers bent in a motel parking lot. The subjects of these

experiments tell a truth about each place they pass through,
and the masters make maps, geographies of affect and emotion.
In an email, my son, living in a city near the North Korean border,

writes that tonight whole families have gathered in his apartment
stairwell, calling ghosts home, burning spirit money. He's attached
a photo that I study, avid, that lonesome for him. In it, a dozen

Chinese couples slow dance in a public park to a jazz band
that plays on and on beneath failing satellites and changing
constellations and the smoke rising from uncounted stairwell fires.

Regarding the Mandala

with my sister and her son
        in the bright and crowded corridor of the museum,
the Buddhist monk and her baby boy see eye-to-eye,
        agreeing that nothing is permanent: not this
sandy sphere of bright, pummeled stone—
        Bound, the docent informs us,
for the churning currents of the Neuse River—not the fine
        curls on that infant head, inclined now
towards the monk who, tools in hand, turns
        away from his work
to stroke the child's curved cheek.

Fire Science

Over whom shall we weep first?
Over the burned ones?

—Morris Rosenfeld

i. The academy

Who pumps? Who ascends
the ladder? Search and rescue?
Wherever you find them, save
them, the slack dummies slumped
over your shoulder. Officers note
each rookie's response as smoke twists
from roof ridge to sun-up sky.
Inside the burn building,
your helmet-light carves dusk
out of darkness. Pry axe, window
punch, and radio weight your belt.
Classroom-perfect to measure
the prowess of its opponents, this fire
behaves in predictable ways.

ii. Exit drill

Everyone moonlights—spreading
seed across the lawns of lawyers,
mending brokers' roofs, pounding
nails, building decks and multilevel dog
houses in doctors' backyards—earnings
under the table, stacked, if you will,

against fingers crushed under the hose-
pack at the warehouse blaze, against
the knee wrenched on ice
at the Christmas tree fire. Strain
and sprain, labor lost. But never you,
stopped cold in the middle of a hot call.

iii. Station house

In between naps and novels, the calls:
overdoses, anytime, day or night, in the flop-
houses by the interstate—each addict
so slight, puddling drool; an auto accident,
the driver wasted on Vicodin
and beer; a trashcan fire in the mall
parking lot, temple sacrifice
under the cold moon. Teenage arsonists.
As you observe the fire licking the wide girth
of the field, they scatter into the woods
on tricked-out bikes. Fuck you.
And you and you.

iv. Incident report

Combustion = Fuel + Heat + Air.
To unlock the chain of events, cordon
off the area. Document the scene.
Interview survivors and note
the locations of the deceased: in closets,
under beds, wrapped in wet towels
in the bathtub, curled around a child's body
in the highest room of the house. Find them—
beyond reproach, remorse, recovery—
skin, fat, muscle, and bone,
all for the flame.

for my brother

Azores Time

Beneath a cracked chandelier cast off
from a job site, my father works wood
with chisel, saw, and awl into a cradle,
a cock-eyed end table, cherry bookends.
Inside his shop, two clocks: east coast
time and the Azores. Watching him,
I remember he had another love
before us. As April dusk smudges the wet,
wet yard he is with her in Fontinhas
again, wild carnivale, flamenco, Graciosa—
glass after glass—loving even the flat, bright
image of the saint she was named for, recalling
the mountain towers where whale-watchers still wait.

      The sea, the sea. It opens inside him,
overflows the yard, the turned beds and birdbath.
Winter's wrens rise in waves around him.

Song of the Last Meeting

after Anna Akhmatova

A conventional woman, I close my eyes
when I kiss, make love under covers. Often,
I can't decide what to wear. It's no accident
I'm alone, teeth chattering, nipples stiff

in the cold. I've rushed out of your car
to the sidewalk at dusk, no coat, no hat. Not
numb, but fully awake. It's done. Roll down
the window and throw me my gloves. I fumble—

right on left, left on right. Please. Go on.
I'm full of this season, brittle leaves
on wind, too much talk, the sun's coy
rays. I know how to find cover, when

to run. Let it end. Winter is a kind of passion
too—a spare house with bare windows.
I breathe deeply, alone, stone beneath
a stuttering bulb, its insistent hum.

Married Man

And later they found him there on the grass,
A pistol near-by tells what had passed.

—"Forsaken Love," A.P. Carter

A hard man from hard people, Newell
travels north from Fancy Gap's knobbed
flank in a highway-stripe yellow Corvette
to an overnight case with Charity attached

to its handles. She's packed panties spritzed
with perfume, nursing texts, a baby-doll
nightgown, and a lady's purse pistol of a serious
caliber. Peaks of Otter Lodge, the Roanoke

Cavalier, Lynchburg Holiday Inn. *So this*
is an affair, she writes in lilac ink. Valedictorian,
lit-mag editor, Charity is a fool for writing.
Rough talk is nothing to him—this in a 29¢

notebook from the college bookstore.
Work-study freshmen that fall, Charity
and I shouldered rolling towers of greasy
dishes into the steam of the dining hall

kitchen, recalling our little sisters and tired
mothers, creepy brothers and distant fathers,
revealing to one another the true color we
wished our hair was. *Two slave-girls,* she writes,

will work for food. After each shift, we pass
St. Jude's bowed sedum, stippled glass,
and river-rock path. *The patron saint of lost causes,*
I explain, my Catholic catechism an exotic

excitement to her Methodist ears. She smiles.
I am a lost cause. In a sure hand, prints,
Sensuality is the grave of the soul. She was one
stop on his bread route, her summer job

at the Galax Motor Diner, where Newell
ordered and Charity served. He had a wife
working the tunnel-oven, second shift at
Merita. He hunted two horny hounds.

She disappeared that spring, her luggage
quietly collected. Then her diaries arrived,
a letter inside: *EXPELLED!! Keep them
safe 'til later. (You know I shot at Newell*

with that damn little gun.) And on the envelope—
Advice for Life: Learn to be generous. Give as good as you get.
Imagine her now, asleep in modest flannel, middle-
aged, in a ranch house on a mountain ridge.

And at her side? Who cares. The wind, the whine
of wheels, the dishwasher's thump: a lullaby
in triple meter, as she dreams the body's
fastnesses, its feints and punts.

Transitions for Dancers
When Dance Is No Longer an Option

For C.D.

You two-step towards me, Charlotte,
     broom in the crook of your arm.
I grab the dustpan, and we clear
     the garage of dead daddy-long-legs,
leaf litter, dog hair, lug a half dozen LPs
     and the record player to the wooden table
next to the washer and dryer, where
     your mother, the lovely Lynda,
former shim-sham queen of Leeds,
     folds and smokes. It's 1968,
and this is not the summer of love.
     Triple-time, bombershay, heel-toe
and cramp-roll—this summer she teaches
     us to tap. Tacks in the heels
and toes of my Keds, I fumble,
     can't quite get it, but you—
your mother's daughter in split-sole
Capezio patent leathers—patter
     and shuffle to "Singing in the Rain."
Though the candidate and his assassin
     make a sad pair on Cronkite,
we've got rhythm, and during one dank week
     learn all the routines from "Stormy

Weather," then "An American in Paris" as French
            students barricade the Sorbonne.
They shout, *Be young and sing out. The old*
            world is behind you—turn to the new.
This is jig plus a stomp, a slave dance driving
            the stiff step of the Irish rover—
picture Shirley Temple and Bojangles on the back lot,
            dancing as if it mattered. Ah, Lynda,
flushed with the fever of a cancer that will kill
            you, you snap off the music in August,
tell us the next steps are not so clear.
            It's only props and poses, after all.
Above the washer, a photo: it's you,
            Lynda, in hungry, damp
England, the decade after the war,
            syncopating across the stage in a trifling
ruffle of pale silk, living for the steady
            thump of applause, a live band,
a warm pint, and a smoke. A stinging wind,
            raw on the throat—smoke,
a signal to the natives, dance.

At the Registry of Regrets

May, the pretzel shop lady, tells me stories,
which are not unlike the pretzels
we bake, wrap, and sell at the mall:
big ones with twists and holes—
and salty, very salty. Stories about her husband,
Sonny—his mother's only boy—
though May calls him Lumpy,
for the crabmeat he plucks from hard
blue-shells at Routten & Rollins by the bay.
    I don't have one yet—
a husband, that is—and May hires me
on the spot. *You need some dough
of your own,* she quips.
    But not this
frozen stuff, I think, shipped weekly
from Likely, West Virginia.
    She shows me
how to dip each pretzel in an acid bath,
arrange them on metal sheets like splayed
soldiers over cold ground. We sell them
for 79 cents to the enlisted men
from the base who are trailed
by docile wives and caterwauling kids,
sell them to the retirees who shop and shop
to shore up a future, to the high school kids
who wander the aisles, empty-fisted.
    Every morning we raise the heavy gate

at the store-front, fire up the black-throated
Vulcan, tip lemonade into the dispenser, rattle
the CO_2 canisters, cram the ice bin, stack
napkins in tidy rows, pour rough salt
and bright mustard into white paper cups
flimsy as tissue flowers and smaller
than a baby's fist.

      "The Bavarian Pretzel" gleams
in neon above the door where May,
cigarette behind one ear, coughs up
grief: her Sonny mows his mother's lawn,
drives his mother to the outlets, and buys her
groceries, a radio for the den. *Sonny can't
forgive*, May says. No sons of his own.
No daughters either.

      Do you know the pretzel? May asks.
I do: medieval, utterly Catholic, a little reward
doled out to good children, a warm pretzel
for piety and fidelity, for lisping the creed,
for prayers humbly recited. The pretzel's
brown loops are folded like a fat
friar's arms before Mass. Its three
holes are Father, Son, and Holy Ghost.

      Cathy, May tells me, *faith makes you stupid.
Or maybe faith makes you sad. Oh, what
the hell*, she says, *you take your pick, girly.*

Teaching Myself to Sew

My father did the sewing in our house—
stripes on his uniform, loose buttons, knee-
patches, hems. After work or before,
he'd gather what was torn. Across
the kitchen table, I'd watch him ply
scissors and thread, a fine needle
between his thumb and thick fingers,
and I'd try to teach myself to sew—
worrying thread through a washrag, basting
uneven rows—but again and again,
my stitching pulled loose from the cloth.
Because I studied his face more closely
than his hands, I never saw how he began,
with that necessary snarl, the knot in the strand.

Sing Whatever Is Well Made

Rain falls from Boston to Baltimore, cascades
    through the Back Bay, across the fens, quarries
and blowy bridges. Our father ropes the luggage to the rack,
    wraps it in plastic, but in my hearth-duster's heart
I know that this week's worth of dirty laundry

    will be rain-soaked, drying stiff and smelly
on the road home. Sister, rain makes us wretched, not just wet,
    as we strap the kids into car seats, drive back south.
My two, your two, murmur in the back. Do you
    remember that ferry we caught after the reunion to leafy,

cool Hingham? It sped from the city, its chewy center,
    past-scene of relatives dead or undone. Jackie the addict,
who died in the Combat Zone, a boy bride. And Donna,
    a rusty redhead, schizophrenic, who showed up
once in faux-fur over fawn freckles. Later, in aloof

    Duxbury, where stern colonials shingle the shore,
we waded chilly shallows, stared past racing
    sails to the working boats, where Papa once worked
lobster and cod, one November left his frozen thumb
    in a trap. My youngest, your youngest, sleep

through the spiraling ramps of the aquarium, built
     by our cousins who climbed steel week-long, smoked
crack after Mass. We cross the Common's lush
     lawns, where our Great-Uncle Ronan, head gardener,
once tended the beds, towed rake and shovel, trowel

     and watering can from end to end. After a glass
or two in Bad Abbott's Bar, Aunt Euena tells more,
     how he drank himself stupid every night,
through seasons of high hope and none, one war, two,
     all his sons gone, his wife a weary nag. He trotted to the track,

blew his wages on lame horses and gloomy women, smacked
     his wife around. But what a hand with the plants!
A wicked assemblage of the ecstatic and awful,
     the heavy-hearted and hopeful, we've carried the past
like a ticking time-bomb to this very day, this reunion

     of the Nova Scotian branch of the clan. In the grand
tradition of my class, I'll wash our shorts and shirts and socks,
     treat the stains that remain, soften pilled fabric. A tender,
a keeper, I'll make it right, sweep the seats, wipe
     the kids' prints from rear windows, point the car home.

Notes

"Patron Saint of the Toothache"

This poem refers to two kinds of saints. The first are the dental students who volunteered at Boston's Forsyth Institute, which was founded in 1910. For more than forty years, the institute provided dental care for Boston's poor and working-class children. The second is Saint Apollonia, patroness saint of dentists and those who suffer toothaches.

"Appetite"

The closing phrase "universal wolf" is Shakespeare's, from *Troilus and Cressida:*

> . . . Power into will, will into appetite;
>
> And appetite, a universal wolf,
>
> So doubly seconded with will and power,
>
> Must make perforce a universal prey,
>
> And last eat up himself.

"Meditation on a Cape Sewn Badly"

The italicized lines are from the novel *Dracula* by Bram Stoker. Throughout the novel, wild dogs and wolves are Count Dracula's minions and familiars, and he controls the animals with simple gestures and verbal commands.

"'You Are Loosed from Your Mooring'"

The title and italicized portion of the last line are taken from Frederick Douglass's *The Narrative of the Life of Frederick Douglass, An American Slave, Written by Himself.*

"A Family I Knew"

The epigraph is taken from Eugenio Cherubini's 1903 novel, *Pinocchio in Africa,* an adaptation—one of hundreds—of Carlo Collodi's well-known children's book *The Adventures of Pinocchio* (1883).

"Geographies of Affect and Emotion"

This poem owes a debt to the insights of scholars and researchers who, in feminist-inflected analyses, have considered how body, emotion, and place work to shape modern consciousness.

"Russian Studies"

This poem samples the poetry of Alexander Blok ("The Twelve"); Osip Mandelstam ("Poem on Stalin"); Anna Akhmatova ("I Wrung My Hands under My Dark Veil"); and references Joseph Brodsky's characterization of Akhmatova as the "keening muse" of twentieth-century Russian history.

"Sing Whatever Is Well Made"

The title of this poem is taken from W. B. Yeats's poem "Under Ben Bulben":

> Irish poets, earn your trade,
> Sing whatever is well made,
> Scorn the sort now growing up
> All out of shape from toe to top,
> Their unremembering hearts and heads
> Base-born products of base beds.
> Sing the peasantry, and then
> Hard-riding country gentlemen,